The Appeals Court of Life

Life

Exploring a Life Sentence

Charles E. Cravey

In His Steps Publishing Company

Disclaimer

This is a work of fiction. Names, characters, places, and incidents are either the product of the author's imagination or used fictitiously. Any resemblance to actual persons, living or deceased, events, or locales is entirely coincidental. The themes and reflections within are intended to inspire, not to instruct or diagnose. The author makes no representations regarding the accuracy of historical or scriptural references, which are woven into the narrative for artistic and devotional purposes.

ISBN: 978-1-58535-049-0 (Paperback)

ISBN: 978-1-58535-073-5 (Kindle)

Library of Congress Catalog Number: 2025917274

Cover design by Book Brush and Charles E. Cravey.

Printed in the United States of America.

Published by In His Steps Publishing, Statesboro, Georgia.

Contents

Preface

"The Appeals Court of Life" employs the framework of a legal appeals court to explore the complexities, challenges, and moral dilemmas we face throughout our lives. Each chapter delves into distinct aspects of human experience, reflecting on how our decisions, actions, and values shape our journeys. The metaphor of the appeals process serves as a powerful tool for examining themes of justice, redemption, personal growth, and the pursuit of truth.

Through this metaphor, readers are invited to consider their own lives as a series of cases brought before an inner tribunal, where every choice is subject to thoughtful reflection and reevaluation. The structure of the book mirrors a legal journey, beginning with the "Opening Statements," where foundational beliefs and early life influences are laid out. As the narrative unfolds, subsequent chapters such as "Evidence and Testimony" investigate the significant relationships and pivotal moments that act as witnesses to our character and integrity.

In "Deliberations," the focus shifts to internal conflicts and the struggle for self-awareness, highlighting the importance of empathy and understanding in reaching fair judgments about ourselves and others. "Verdicts and Sentences" considers the consequences of our actions, emphasizing accountability and the possibility of transformation through learning from past mistakes.

The closing chapters offer hope and encourage resilience, underscoring the idea that life grants us opportunities to revise our paths and seek redemption. By navigating through the intricacies of this metaphorical courtroom, we are encouraged to embrace personal growth, achieving a deeper sense of fulfillment and wisdom in the journey of life.

Chapter 1

Self-Reflection

"The law is reason, free from passion." —*Aristotle*

Self-reflection is an essential aspect of personal growth, enabling individuals to assess their decisions and actions, understand their motivations, and confront their regrets. Characters in literature often engage in self-reflection, allowing readers to witness the complexities of human behavior and decision-making. This exploration can manifest through various forms, including internal monologues, dialogues with other characters, and symbolic actions that reveal a character's deeper thoughts and feelings.

One notable example is Jay Gatsby from F. Scott Fitzgerald's "The Great Gatsby." Gatsby's relentless pursuit of his idealized past with Daisy Buchanan illustrates a profound struggle with regret. His attempts to recapture a moment that has long since passed lead him to make questionable choices, culminating in his tragic fate. In moments of self-reflection, Gatsby does not fully grasp the impact of his decisions on himself and those around him. His desire to "repeat the past" serves as both an appeal to reclaim lost love and a refusal to confront the reality of his present circumstances, highlighting the tensions between ambition and regret.

Similarly, the character of Ebenezer Scrooge in Charles Dickens' "A Christmas Carol" undergoes a profound transformation through self-reflection. After being visited by the ghosts of Christmas Past, Present, and Yet to Come, Scrooge is forced to confront the consequences of his selfish actions and the isolation he has created for himself. His journey reflects an appeal against the regrets of his life, as he chooses to embrace generosity and connection. Scrooge's internal assessment leads him to seek redemption, underscoring the possibility of change and the importance of self-awareness.

In a more contemporary context, stories often feature protagonists who grapple with the consequences of their choices in an environment that demands quick decision-making. For example, in Khaled Hosseini's "The Kite Runner," Amir's childhood decisions lead to profound guilt and a desire for redemption. His self-reflection throughout the novel becomes a means of appealing against the wrongs he has committed, as he seeks to atone for his past actions by returning to Afghanistan and standing up against his regrets. This journey highlights the theme of personal responsibility and the complexity of navigating guilt and redemption.

In literature, characters' moments of self-reflection often serve as pivotal turning points that propel them toward growth and change. Whether through regret or a desire for redemption, these reflections can illuminate the intricacies of human nature, fostering empathy in readers and prompting them to consider their own choices. By exploring the depth of these characters' journeys, we are reminded of the importance of self-assessment and the potential for transformation that lies in confronting our past. Literature provides a rich tapestry for examining how individuals navigate the landscape of their decisions and the continuous quest to reconcile their actions with their sense of self.

Whether in classic literature or modern narratives, self-reflection remains a powerful tool for character development, offering insights into the human condition. As readers, we are invited to journey alongside these characters, witnessing their struggles and triumphs, and finding echoes of our own experiences within their stories. This exploration not only enriches our understanding of the characters but also encourages us to engage in our own self-reflective practices. Through these literary mirrors, we are reminded that growth often requires vulnerability and the courage to face our own truths. In doing so, we open the door to transformation, allowing us to craft narratives of change and hope in our own lives. Thus, literature serves as both a reflection and a catalyst, inspiring us to become more introspective and compassionate individuals.

As we delve into these narratives, we are reminded that the journey of self-reflection is not a solitary path but rather one that resonates with the collective human experience. It is a tapestry woven with threads of introspection, empathy, and resilience. By examining the inner workings of characters who confront their past, embrace their flaws, and strive for a better future, we are offered a roadmap to navigate our own complexities.

The power of self-reflection in literature lies in its ability to foster connection—not only with the characters but also within us. It challenges us to question, to learn, and to grow. It nudges us to consider the legacy of our actions and the impact we have on the world around us. These stories remind us that while the past cannot be changed, the future is full of possibilities waiting to be shaped by our newfound insights and commitments to personal growth.

In this way, literature becomes a timeless companion, guiding us through the ebbs and flows of life, urging us to look inward and outward with renewed understanding and compassion. It is through these reflective journeys that we find the courage to rewrite our own stories, embracing the transformative power of self-awareness and the profound potential for change.

As we turn the pages of these narratives, we are not merely passive observers; we are active participants in a shared exploration of the human spirit. Each character's introspection invites us to confront our own narratives, to question our motives, and to ponder the consequences of our actions. This literary engagement enriches our lives, offering both comfort and challenge, as it compels us to confront the truths we sometimes hesitate to face.

In embracing the lessons woven into these stories, we learn that self-reflection is not an endpoint but a journey—a continuous process of becoming. It teaches us that vulnerability is not a weakness but a strength, enabling us to connect more deeply with others and ourselves. By understanding the characters we encounter, we gain insights into our own hopes, fears, and aspirations.

Thus, literature serves as a mirror, reflecting not only the complexities of its characters but also the intricacies of our own lives. It encourages us to strive for authenticity, to live with intention, and to seek out the beauty in our imperfections. Through this shared journey of reflection and growth, we find solace in the knowledge that we are not alone—that our struggles and triumphs resonate with the universal human experience, binding us together in our quest for meaning and fulfillment.

Chapter 2

Judgment and Forgiveness

"An unjust law is no law at all." —St. Augustine

Judgment is an inherent part of the human experience, often serving as a mechanism for navigating the complexities of our relationships and interactions. When we judge ourselves, we engage in an internal dialogue that shapes our self-perception and self-worth. This self-judgment can manifest in various forms: we might critique our decisions, berate ourselves for past mistakes, or hold ourselves to unattainable standards. Such judgments can lead to feelings of guilt, shame, or inadequacy, building walls that isolate us from self-acceptance and growth.

Similarly, when we judge others, we typically do so through the lens of our values, beliefs, and experiences. This external judgment often stems from our desire to uphold moral standards or to understand behaviors that differ from our own. However, it's essential to recognize that judgment can easily shift into harsh criticism or prejudice, leading to division and conflict. The tendency to judge others can prevent us from fostering empathy, understanding, and compassion, both for ourselves and those around us.

The interplay between judgment and forgiveness becomes crucial in this context. Forgiveness—both of ourselves and others—can be a transformative act that allows us to move beyond the constraints of judgment. Self-forgiveness involves acknowledging our imperfections and mistakes without allowing them to define us. It requires a gentle re-evaluation of our self-judgment, shifting from blame to understanding. By practicing self-forgiveness, we can cultivate resilience and emotional well-being, recognizing that we are all fallible beings on a continuous journey of learning and growth.

Forgiving others is equally important, facilitating the release of grudges and resentment that can burden our hearts. When we choose to forgive, we acknowledge the pain caused by others' actions but also affirm our commitment to healing and moving forward. This act can break the cycle of judgment, fostering a sense of empathy that allows us to view others through a lens of understanding rather than condemnation. It invites us to see their humanity, recognizing that we, too, are flawed and capable of error.

To judge ourselves and others is to grapple with the complexities of our shared humanity. However, the path of forgiveness offers a route to transcend judgment, enabling us to approach ourselves and others with compassion. It encourages a deeper understanding of our experiences and struggles, fostering a spirit of connectedness. Ultimately, embracing both judgment and forgiveness enriches our relationships, allowing us to grow and heal in ways that affirm our collective journey through life.

By integrating judgment and forgiveness into our lives, we embark on a transformative journey toward greater self-awareness and interpersonal harmony. This balance not only nurtures our personal development but also enhances our connections with others, creating a more compassionate and inclusive environment. As we practice these principles, we come to appreciate the profound impact they have on our emotional and mental well-being.

Moreover, cultivating a mindset that embraces forgiveness can lead to positive ripple effects throughout our communities. When we model forgiveness, we inspire others to do the same, fostering a culture of understanding and acceptance. This cultural shift can diminish hostility and promote peaceful coexistence, as individuals learn to navigate differences with grace and empathy.

The dance between judgment and forgiveness is an ongoing process that requires patience and intentionality. It challenges us to confront our biases and predispositions, urging us to grow beyond them. As we strive to balance these elements, we not only enrich our own lives but also contribute to a more harmonious and compassionate world.

In this way, judgment and forgiveness serve not just as personal tools, but as powerful catalysts for broader societal change. They remind us that while we may falter, the capacity for growth and redemption is always within reach, allowing us to forge a path toward a kinder, more understanding future.

Examples of this can be seen in various aspects of our lives, from personal relationships to societal movements. In personal relationships, for instance, couples who practice forgiveness often find that their bonds strengthen over time. By choosing to forgive each other's shortcomings and missteps, they build a foundation of trust and resilience, enabling them to navigate challenges with grace and understanding.

In the larger societal context, movements centered around restorative justice exemplify the transformative power of forgiveness. These initiatives seek to repair harm by fostering dialogue between offenders and victims, promoting healing rather than retribution. This approach not only helps individuals reconcile and move forward but also contributes to a more equitable justice system that prioritizes rehabilitation over punishment.

Furthermore, communities that have embraced reconciliation efforts after conflict provide compelling examples of forgiveness in action. By acknowledging past grievances and working collaboratively toward healing, such communities have been able to overcome division and build a more cohesive, inclusive environment.

These examples highlight how the principles of judgment and forgiveness can extend beyond the individual, influencing the fabric of society and encouraging a culture of empathy and understanding. As we continue to apply these principles in our lives, we contribute to the creation of a world where compassion and growth are prioritized, paving the way for a brighter, more harmonious future.

To accomplish the creation of a world grounded in compassion and growth, it begins with individual commitment and collective action. Here are some steps we can take to foster this transformation:

1. **Education and Awareness:** By integrating emotional intelligence and empathy training into educational systems, we can equip future generations with the tools to navigate their emotions and relationships constructively. This foundation nurtures a society that values understanding over judgment.

2. **Community Engagement:** Encourage open dialogues within communities, creating spaces where diverse perspectives are heard and respected. Community events, workshops, and forums can help bridge gaps and foster

a sense of belonging and mutual respect.

3. **Role Modeling:** Leaders and influencers can play a pivotal role by exemplifying forgiveness and empathy in their actions and decisions. When those in positions of power demonstrate these values, it sets a standard that others are likely to follow.

4. **Encouraging Restorative Practices:** Adopt restorative justice practices in workplaces and institutions, promoting healing and reconciliation rather than punishment. This shift can transform conflict resolution into opportunities for growth and understanding.

5. **Mindfulness and Reflection:** Encourage practices such as mindfulness and meditation, which help individuals cultivate self-awareness and regulate their emotional responses. This personal growth translates into more compassionate interactions with others.

6. **Policy and Advocacy:** Advocate for policies that support mental health, conflict resolution, and community building. By creating systems that prioritize well-being and inclusivity, we lay the groundwork for a more empathetic society.

7. **Celebrating Diversity:** Celebrate and learn from cultural, ethnic, and ideological differences, recognizing that diversity enriches our communities. Promoting intercultural exchanges and collaborations can enhance mutual understanding and cooperation.

8. **Narrative Change:** Use media and storytelling to highlight stories of forgiveness and compassion, challenging dominant narratives of division and hostility. Positive stories can inspire others to act with kindness and empathy.

By taking these steps, we each play a role in weaving a tapestry of kindness and hope that extends beyond ourselves, shaping a future where empathy and understanding are at the heart of societal interactions. This transformative journey, while challenging, offers the promise of a world where every individual feels valued and connected.

An example of this would be the way schools are beginning to integrate social and emotional learning (SEL) into their curricula. By teaching students skills such as empathy, active listening, and conflict resolution, educators are laying the groundwork for a generation that approaches differences with compassion rather than judgment. These lessons go beyond traditional academic subjects, equipping young people with the tools they need to navigate a complex world with grace and understanding.

Similarly, initiatives that focus on community storytelling have proven to be powerful examples of fostering empathy and connection. Programs that encourage individuals to share their personal stories, particularly those from marginalized communities, help break down stereotypes and build bridges of understanding. By listening to the diverse experiences of others, participants are prompted to reflect on their own biases and judgments, creating a ripple effect of empathy that can transform communities.

In the realm of international relations, truth and reconciliation commissions serve as another poignant example. By addressing historical injustices and providing a platform for victims and perpetrators to voice their experiences, these commissions aim to heal deep societal wounds and promote national unity. The process acknowledges past harms while paving the way for a future built on mutual respect and understanding.

These examples demonstrate the profound impact that prioritizing judgment and forgiveness can have, not only on individual lives but also on the broader societal fabric. As we each commit to

these principles, we contribute to a legacy of compassion and inclusivity, ensuring that future generations inherit a world where
kindness prevails over division.

Chapter 3

The Opinion of Others

"The good of the people is the highest law." —*Cicero*

An Example:

In a small town, where everyone knew each other's business, two distinct families—the Carters and the Nguyens—found themselves at odds over a community park project. The Carters, a traditionally conservative family led by John, believed in preserving the park's natural state, while the Nguyens, who had recently moved into the area, envisioned a vibrant space filled with playgrounds and community gardens.

Lily Carter stood at the edge of the park, her heart pounding as she watched her father engage in animated discussions with neighbors. The whispers around her felt like sharp daggers. "Who do they think they are, coming in and changing everything?" one voice echoed. It gnawed at her, the implication that her family was somehow less than, that their values were outdated. Lily felt the weight of those opinions, shaping her own perceptions of fairness and justice.

Across the park, Khoa Nguyen observed the same scene through a different lens. His family had faced scorn since their arrival, the unfamiliarity of their culture casting them as outsiders. He had overheard comments about how they didn't belong, how their ideas were un-American. Yet, he couldn't shake the feeling that their vision was revolutionary—a chance to bring the community together. Still, every time someone scoffed at their suggestions, he felt a flicker of doubt seep in. What if they were right?

As days turned into weeks, the community meetings grew more heated. Each family represented not just their own interests but unknowingly became symbols of larger societal divides. Lily and

Khoa, frustrated and confused, found themselves at a makeshift table one evening, eyes locked in an acknowledgment that transcended their families' rivalry. They shared their burdens—the stares, the harsh words, and the silent judgments.

"Do you ever feel like everyone's watching us?" Lily asked, her voice barely above a whisper.

Khoa nodded, his eyes reflecting the agony of being dissected by those around them. "Yeah. It's like we have to fight against everyone else's opinions before we can even figure out what we want."

Suddenly, the two felt united against a common foe—the external opinions that distorted their views of justice and fairness. They devised a plan to bridge their differences, determined that the park could embody both preservation and progress, and merged nature with community.

When they presented their combined proposal at the next community meeting, they were met with a wall of skepticism. "How can you two collaborate?" a voice shouted from the back. "You stand for completely different things!"

But instead of cowering, Lily and Khoa stood firm. They shared their personal stories, how they felt judged, and what fairness meant to them. They laid bare the complexities of identity shaped by external perceptions.

Slowly, the crowd began to shift. Families started to share their own experiences of feeling judged, revealing a tapestry of misunderstandings woven through the community. It became clear that their righteousness in holding onto their beliefs had created a chasm, not a unity.

As discussions continued, the characters found themselves strengthened by the understanding that others' opinions, while influential, didn't have to define them. Instead, they wielded their narratives like shields, drawing people in rather than pushing them away. With solidarity building, they proposed a creative initiative—a community mural reflecting both nature and cultural diversity that would stand as a testament to their collaboration.

When the mural was completed, the community marveled at the vivid scenes that wrapped around the park's old oak tree. Not only did it symbolize preservation and innovation, but it also became a canvas for conversations about fairness and justice.

In the end, the characters realized that while the opinions of others had once weighed heavily on them, they could also be a source of connection and growth. The park became not just a space for play but a sanctuary of understanding, where stories merged and judgments were left at the gate. They had redefined their sense of justice, focusing inward rather than outward, forging a path toward a more inclusive and compassionate community.

As Lily and Khoa walked through the newly transformed park, they exchanged smiles. They had navigated the tides of judgment, emerging with a deeper understanding of justice that embraced the voices of many rather than the singular view of a few. They learned that external opinions could shape their paths, but it was their shared values and empathy that created true fairness.

The park, once a battleground of competing visions, now stood as a vibrant testament to unity and resilience. Children laughed and played on the swings and slides, while nearby, community gardens thrived under the care of volunteers from all levels of society. The mural, a kaleidoscope of colors and stories, drew visitors in, inviting them to see the world through multiple perspectives.

Lily and Khoa often visited the park together, their friendship a symbol of what was possible when differences were embraced rather than feared. They continued to share their journey with

others, inspiring new conversations about community and acceptance. The park had become more than just a place—it was
a living symbol of what could be achieved when people listened,
learned, and grew together.

In this small town, where once everyone knew only each other's
business, they now knew each other's stories, dreams, and hopes.
The Carters and the Nguyens had not just changed a park; they
had ignited a movement towards understanding and kindness.
And in doing so, they taught their town that compassion and
collaboration were the keys to true progress, ensuring that every
voice, no matter how different, was heard and cherished.

The opinion of others, whether we think so or not, makes a
significant difference in our lives. It can shape our decisions, influence our self-esteem, and even alter the course of our future
endeavors. However, as Lily and Khoa discovered, the power of
these opinions lies not in their ability to define us, but in our
response to them.

When opinions felt like chains, holding them to outdated beliefs
or foreign expectations, they realized the liberation that comes
from choosing their own path. By embracing their unique per-

spectives and fostering dialogue, they transformed what might have been an insurmountable divide into a bridge of understanding.

In our own lives, we can learn from Lily and Khoa's journey. By listening to the opinions of others, we gain insight into different perspectives and challenge our own assumptions. Yet, it's vital to remember that we are not obligated to conform to these views. Instead, we can use them as a tool for growth, shaping our own narratives that resonate with our core values and aspirations.

The true measure of success lies not in the approval of others, but in the fulfillment of our potential and the strength of our connections. As we navigate the ebb and flow of external judgment, may we find the courage to honor our authentic selves, contributing to a world where diversity is celebrated and empathy reigns supreme.

In this ever-evolving tapestry of human experience, the stories of Lily and Khoa serve as a gentle reminder of the transformative power of empathy and open-mindedness. Their journey teaches us that even in the face of adversity and misunderstanding, we can create spaces where voices of all kinds can coexist harmoniously.

Let us strive to cultivate environments where acceptance and inclusivity are not just ideals but realities. When we welcome dialogue and embrace differences, we pave the way for richer, more meaningful interactions. By doing so, we not only honor the individuality of each person but also weave a stronger, more resilient community fabric.

May we carry forward the lessons learned from this small town, using them as a beacon to guide our own interactions. As we engage with the world, let us nurture a spirit of kindness and cooperation, understanding that through unity, we can achieve remarkable things. Together, we can build a future where every person feels valued, every story is heard, and every dream has the space to flourish.

Chapter 4

Life on Trial

Cases of Growth and Resilience

"The first duty of society is justice." —Alexander Hamilton

Introduction: The Courtroom of Life

Opening Statement: The premise of life is a courtroom, where every significant event is a trial that tests our character, resilience, and commitment to personal growth. We must establish the importance of examining these "cases" not only to understand our past but to prepare for future challenges.

In this courtroom, the jury is composed of our experiences, and the verdicts are the insights we draw from them. This book is your guide through these trials, each chapter a case study that dissects the complexities of human experience. Together, we will explore how life's adversities can transform into opportunities for growth, resilience, and self-discovery.

- **Setting the Stage:** Life's unpredictable nature often presents scenarios that feel like legal proceedings, where we must present evidence of our perseverance and adaptability. These experiences, though daunting, are crucial in shaping who we are. Through the cases presented in this book, you will see how each challenge is not just an obstacle but a steppingstone toward a more resilient self.

- **Purpose of the Journey:** This exploration aims to empower you to become your own advocate in the courtroom of life. By understanding and embracing the trials you face, you gain the tools necessary for personal evolution. The stories and insights shared here will encourage you to reflect on your own life, recognizing that each trial is an essential part of your journey toward growth and fulfillment.

Let us embark on this journey together, examining the trials of life as opportunities to learn, grow, and emerge stronger. Welcome to the courtroom of life, where every case is an opportunity for transformation.

The Case of the Lost Job

Setting the Scene: On the day the job was lost, it felt as though the gavel of fate had come down hard, signaling a pivotal moment in the courtroom of life. The air was thick with tension, as the unexpected news delivered a blow that resonated deeply. Stress, confusion, and fear took the stand, each presenting their case with relentless fervor. The evidence was overwhelming—sleepless nights, worried glances, and the haunting question of "What now?" lingered in the air like a shadow.

- **Key Testimonies:** Friends and family stepped forward to offer their testimonies, recounting the emotional impact they witnessed. A close friend recalled the initial shock, describing it as a storm that swallowed hope. A family member, with compassion in their voice, spoke of the quiet strength observed in moments of vulnerability, highlighting the resilience that began to emerge despite the turmoil. Their words painted a picture of a support network that, while shaken, remained steadfast, providing a foundation upon which new beginnings could be built.

- **Verdict:** As the trial unfolded, a quiet realization began to take root. The loss, initially perceived as a devastating defeat, gradually revealed itself as a catalyst for transformation. Freed from the confines of a role that no longer served, hidden passions and dormant skills started to surface, like seeds breaking through soil to reach the light. This unexpected journey, though unchosen, became an opportunity to explore new paths and redefine what success truly meant. In the end, the verdict was clear: the loss was not an end, but rather a crucial turning point on the road to self-discovery and renewed purpose.

The Case of Broken Relationships

Opening Argument:

In the courtroom of life, the breakdown of a relationship stands as one of the most profound trials we may face. These experiences often come with their own charges of heartache, disappointment, and regret, yet they also hold the potential for immense personal growth. Just as in any trial, the outcome largely depends on how we choose to interpret and respond to the proceedings. Will we allow the bitterness of a broken bond to dictate our future, or will we embrace the opportunity to learn and evolve?

- ## Examination of Witnesses:

To utterly understand the intricacies of a broken relationship, we must examine the testimonies of those intimately involved. Former partners offer valuable insights, each presenting their perspective on the dynamics that once existed. One might speak of communication missteps, while another highlights unmet needs or differing life goals. Close friends, observing from the sidelines, provide their own reflections, noting changes in demeanor or the subtle signs of growing apart. Through these diverse narratives, a clearer picture emerges, showing how individual experiences intertwine to shape the collective narrative.

- **Ruling:**

As the case unfolds, the ruling becomes apparent: the end of a relationship, though painful, is not without purpose. These experiences teach us resilience, urging us to examine what we truly value in our connections with others. They offer clarity, helping us define boundaries and prioritize compatibility and mutual respect in future relationships. In the end, we gain the wisdom to approach new relationships with a deeper understanding of ourselves and a renewed commitment to nurturing connections that align with our authentic selves. This trial, though challenging, guides us toward healthier, more fulfilling relationships in the future.

The Case of Illness

Indictment of Fear:

In the courtroom of life, few trials are as daunting as the case of illness. When faced with a serious medical diagnosis, fear and uncertainty stand as the primary charges, casting a long shadow over one's existence. The mind races with questions, each one more unsettling than the last: "What does this mean for my future?" "How will my life change?" These fears, palpable and profound, demand to be acknowledged, as they often dictate the initial stages of the journey through illness.

- **Expert Testimony:**

To navigate this complex trial, we turn to expert testimonies from medical professionals and counselors who illuminate the psychological landscape of illness and recovery. A doctor may speak to the physical realities, detailing treatment options and expected outcomes, while a counselor explores the emotional and mental resilience required to face such a challenge. Together, they help construct a comprehensive understanding of the journey, emphasizing the importance of a supportive network and the power of a positive mindset in overcoming the hurdles ahead.

- **Final Judgment:**

As the trial progresses, a transformation often takes place. The initial fear, once overwhelming, begins to give way to a sense of empowerment and resilience. Through the struggle and recovery, individuals frequently discover a newfound gratitude for life, cherishing moments once taken for granted. This journey, though arduous, instills a deeper appreciation for health and well-being, prompting a commitment to nurturing both the body and the spirit. In the end, the verdict is not merely one of survival, but of profound personal growth and an enriched perspective on life. This case, like so many others in the courtroom of life, reinforces the truth that trials, though challenging, are pivotal to our evolution.

The Case of Major Life Transitions

- **Context of Change:**

In the grand courtroom of life, major transitions stand as pivotal cases that test our adaptability and courage. Whether it's moving to a new city, starting a new career, or stepping into the role of a parent, these transitions are laden with both challenges and opportunities for growth. Just as any trial demands careful navigation, so too do these life changes require us to present evidence of our resilience and readiness to adapt. Each transition is a testament to the dynamic nature of life, urging us to embrace change as an integral part of our personal journey.

- **Witness Statements:**

To understand the breadth of these transitions, we turn to personal anecdotes from those who have walked similar paths. A colleague recounts the excitement and trepidation of relocating to a bustling city, where every street and face was unfamiliar. They highlight the importance of building new connections and finding a sense of belonging amidst the chaos. Meanwhile, a new parent shares the overwhelming mix of joy and responsibility that accompanies the arrival of a child, emphasizing the profound shift in priorities and identity. These witnesses paint a vivid picture of the varied reactions and adaptations that major life transitions evoke, each narrative offering unique insights into the human capacity for change.

- **Outcome:**

As we examine these cases, the outcome becomes clear: embracing change is a critical aspect of personal evolution. Each transition, though daunting, serves as a catalyst for growth, pushing us beyond our comfort zones and into new realms of possibility. By facing these trials head-on, we learn to cultivate flexibility, resilience, and a deeper understanding of ourselves. In the end, the verdict in the courtroom of life is one of empowerment. These transitions, far from being mere disruptions, become steppingstones that lead us toward a more fulfilling and authentic existence. Through them, we discover the strength to navigate life's uncertainties and the wisdom to appreciate the journey itself.

The Case of Failure

Charge of Disappointment:

In the courtroom of life, failure is a formidable opponent, often serving as a daunting charge brought against us. It stands in the witness box, armed with evidence of struggles, doubts, and perceived inadequacies, each piece meticulously presented during the introspective trial of self-reflection. The weight of disappointment can feel overwhelming, casting a shadow over our achievements and aspirations. Yet, as with any case, it is how we respond to these charges that defines the outcome.

- **Character Witness:**

Enter the character witnesses—mentors and role models who have navigated their own tumultuous journeys through failure. They share their stories, illustrating how setbacks were not endpoints but rather turning points on the path to personal growth. A beloved teacher recounts a failed project that, while initially devastating, became the catalyst for innovation and perseverance. A respected leader describes how early career missteps taught invaluable lessons in humility and resilience, shaping them into the person they are today. These testimonies offer hope and guidance, underscoring the truth that failure is not a final verdict, but a necessary chapter in the quest for success.

- **Judgment:**

As the trial progresses, a powerful judgment emerges: failures, while challenging, are integral to the journey of personal development and resilience. Each misstep provides a unique learning opportunity, teaching us patience, adaptability, and the courage to try again. Through failure, we gain clarity on our strengths and weaknesses, allowing for more informed decisions and a deeper understanding of ourselves. The courtroom of life reveals that failure is not an indictment of our worth, but rather a stepping-stone toward greater achievements. In the end, the verdict is one of empowerment—embracing failure as a transformative force that propels us forward, fortifying our resolve and enriching our path to growth.

The Case of Triumph

Opening Statement of Victory:

In the courtroom of life, triumph stands as a testament to our perseverance and determination. These moments of success are the victories that deserve to be celebrated and cherished. Each positive outcome, no matter how small, is a powerful reminder of our capabilities and the potential that lies within us. Just as trials are analyzed for the lessons they impart, so too are victories, for they provide the motivation and confidence needed to face future challenges with renewed vigor.

- **Witnesses of Celebration:**

The joy of success is often magnified by the presence of those who supported us along the way. Friends, family, and mentors gather as witnesses to our triumphs, their cheers and encouragement echoing through the halls of our journey. A beloved mentor may recount the dedication and hard work that led to this moment of victory, highlighting the determination witnessed firsthand. Family members, beaming with pride, speak of the relentless effort and sacrifices made, underscoring the strength and resilience that have defined the path to success. These supporters, each with their own narrative of shared joy, enrich the experience, transforming personal achievement into a collective celebration.

- **Final Verdict:**

As we reflect on these victories, the final verdict becomes clear: recognizing and celebrating our successes is essential for ongoing growth. These moments are not merely endpoints but crucial milestones, marking progress in the journey of personal development. By acknowledging our triumphs, we reinforce our belief in ourselves and our ability to overcome obstacles. They serve as beacons of motivation, illuminating the path ahead and reminding us that, no matter the trials we may face, triumph is always within reach. In the courtroom of life, these victories are not just moments of joy but vital components of the narrative that shapes our evolving story.

Conclusion: The Ongoing Trial of Life

Life, much like an unfolding courtroom drama, presents us with a series of trials that never truly end. Each chapter of our lives writes itself as a new case, filled with its own challenges and revelations. These trials, though often daunting, are the crucibles through which our character is forged, and our resilience is tested. They teach us, mold us, and prepare us for what lies ahead. It is crucial to understand that these experiences are not isolated incidents but interconnected threads that weave the complex tapestry of our existence.

- **Encouragement:**

As we close this exploration of life's trials, let us take a moment to appreciate the journey we've traversed. Remember, each past trial was a necessary step on the path to who you are today and who you will become tomorrow. Embrace these experiences, for they are the building blocks of personal evolution. The jury of self-acceptance and resilience is, indeed, in your hands. You have the power to view each trial not as an insurmountable obstacle but as an opportunity for growth and enlightenment.

Every moment of adversity you have faced has equipped you with unique insights and strengths. Carry this wisdom forward and wield it like a beacon to guide you through future challenges. As you continue your journey, remain steadfast in the belief that you are your own best advocate in the courtroom of life. With courage and conviction, step into each new case, knowing that you possess the resilience and tenacity to emerge stronger on the other side.

Epilogue: Reflections from the Bench

As we reach the epilogue, we step back to take stock of the journey through the courtroom of life. Here, we find ourselves on the bench, reflecting on the tapestry of trials that have shaped us. Resilience and personal growth are not finite achievements but ongoing processes, much like a series of cases that demand our attention and introspection. Each trial, whether it brings triumph or tribulation, contributes to our evolving understanding of ourselves and the world around us.

In this reflection, it's vital to recognize that the power to navigate life's complexities lies within us. We are not merely witnesses to our lives but active participants, capable of shaping our narratives with intention and insight. As your own advocate, you can approach each challenge with a mindset geared toward growth, extracting lessons and cultivating wisdom from every experience.

Remember, the courtroom of personal development is always open, ready to welcome the next case. Embrace each new opportunity with curiosity and courage, knowing that the path to resilience is paved with both successes and setbacks. As you continue your journey, may you find strength in your trials, joy in your victories, and peace in the knowledge that every step forward is a testament to your enduring spirit. Here's to the perpetual trial of life and the boundless potential it holds for transformation and self-discovery.

Chapter 5

Community vs. Individual

"It is better that ten guilty persons escape than that one innocent suffer." —William Blackstone

"Threads of Belonging"

Main Plot:

The story centers around two characters in a small, close-knit town—Elena and Jonah. Elena is the daughter of the town's revered mayor, and her whole life has been spent under the spotlight of community expectations. From a young age, she's been groomed to take over her father's role, with everyone in the town holding her to the standard of perfection. On the other hand, Jonah is an aspiring artist who feels stifled by the town's conservative values. He yearns for freedom and a chance to explore his creativity beyond the town's limitations.

Both Elena and Jonah navigate their lives amidst the unyielding pressures of tradition and the desire for self-expression. As Elena grapples with the weight of her predetermined path, she often finds solace in her secret notebook, where her unsung songs dwell. Each page bears the whispers of her heart, yearning to break free from the mold that her family and community have cast for her.

Jonah, meanwhile, spends his days wandering the fields and forests surrounding the town, sketchbook in hand. He captures the world as he sees it, raw and unfiltered, in the hope that one day his art will be understood and appreciated for its authenticity rather than its adherence to convention.

Their worlds intertwine when they meet at a local festival. It's a chance encounter that sparks an unexpected friendship. Through their shared experiences and dreams, they find encouragement in one another's company, igniting a spark of rebellion against the constraints that bind them.

As they grow closer, Elena and Jonah become each other's confidants, sharing their deepest fears and aspirations. They begin to challenge each other to step out of the shadows of expectation and into the light of their true selves. This journey is not without its challenges, as they face criticism and doubt from those around them, yet they find strength in their bond, determined to reshape their destinies.

Subplot:

As the main plot unfolds, we see both characters face pivotal decisions shaped by societal norms. Elena, deeply ingrained in her role, feels the pressure to conform. She hesitates to pursue her passion for writing songs because it doesn't align with the community's expectations of her future. Her journey reflects the struggle for validation—she often finds herself rehearsing speeches for her father's events instead of exploring her own voice, leaving her feeling unfulfilled.

However, a turning point comes when Elena stumbles upon an old journal belonging to her grandmother, a woman she always admired but never truly understood. The journal reveals stories of rebellion, courage, and a hidden passion for music that her grandmother had never shared with the world. This discovery ignites a spark within Elena, making her realize that the desire to express oneself authentically runs in her family. It becomes a source of inspiration and strength, encouraging her to reconsider her path.

Meanwhile, Jonah faces a different challenge. His mentor, an older artist who once left the town to pursue a career in the city, returns for a visit. The mentor shares tales of struggles and triumphs in the broader art world, but also emphasizes the importance of staying true to one's vision. This conversation encourages Jonah to value his unique perspective and to see the potential impact his artwork could have, not just beyond the town's borders, but within it as well.

Together, these newfound insights propel Elena and Jonah to take bold steps toward their dreams. Elena begins composing songs that blend her community's traditional melodies with her own modern style, creating a unique sound that speaks to people's hearts. Jonah, inspired by his mentor and Elena's courage, begins to paint with even more passion, incorporating elements of the town's history into his abstract works, allowing the community to see their own stories reflected in his art.

As they embrace their individual paths, both Elena and Jonah gradually influence those around them. Their courage to defy expectations and follow their passions becomes a beacon of hope for others in the town, sparking a quiet revolution of self-expression and acceptance.

Meanwhile, Jonah battles his urge to create art inspired by the outside world versus painting what the community deems acceptable. He receives relentless criticism for his abstract pieces, which appear foreign to the traditional perspectives held by many townspeople. The local art show looms, and he contemplates whether to showcase pieces that conform to the community's tastes or to present his true self, risking rejection.

Throughout the story, flashbacks reveal moments when Elena sought validation from her peers rather than embracing her individuality. A pivotal scene occurs when Elena overhears her friends discussing her possible future. They urge her to marry a local suitor and take up community duties, solidifying her choice to conform instead of choosing her own dreams. This moment sends her spiraling into self-doubt.

In contrast, Jonah eventually gathers the courage to host an underground art exhibit. His decision comes after a bonding moment with Elena over their mutual struggles. They encourage each other to embrace their authenticity rather than succumb to societal pressures. The exhibit becomes a symbol of rebellion against conventional norms. As Jonah's art challenges the community to reconsider their definition of beauty and expression, Elena slowly finds the courage to share her songs with the world.

Together, they create a space where vulnerability is celebrated and authenticity is championed. Jonah's underground exhibit is held in an old, abandoned barn on the outskirts of town, a place where whispers of the past mingle with the daring voices of the present. As the evening unfolds, the barn is filled with a diverse tapestry of people—artists, dreamers, and even those who once doubted the merit of such bold expressions.

The walls are adorned with Jonah's artwork, each piece a narrative of defiance and hope. The vibrant colors and evocative forms speak to the soul, inviting viewers to see the world through Jonah's eyes. For many, it's a revelation—a moment where they begin to question the constraints they have always accepted as immovable.

Elena, standing amidst the crowd, feels a surge of confidence. Encouraged by Jonah's bravery, she steps onto a makeshift stage at the center of the barn. With a deep breath, she begins to sing her original song—a heartfelt melody that captures the essence of her journey and the longing for true belonging. Her voice, though slightly trembling at first, gains strength with each note, wrapping around the audience like a warm embrace.

As her song comes to an end, there's a moment of silence—a collective intake of breath—before applause erupts, echoing off the barn walls. It's a moment of triumph, not just for Elena and Jonah, but for the entire community. Those who once resisted change find themselves moved by the raw honesty of the evening, realizing that there is beauty in diversity and strength in authenticity.

The exhibit and Elena's performance mark the beginning of a transformation within the town. Conversations shift, and the rigid boundaries of tradition begin to blur, making way for a more inclusive and understanding community. Both Jonah and Elena learn that by embracing their true selves, they have ignited a spark that has the power to illuminate the lives of others, proving that sometimes, the most profound changes start with a single act of courage.

Climactic Twist:

When the night of Jonah's exhibit arrives, the community is divided between those who are drawn to the rawness of his art and those who are outraged. During this tension, Elena publicly shares her first song, which speaks to the heart of their struggles with identity and belonging. Her vulnerability resonates with many in the audience, stirring a wave of emotional responses, and serving as a catalyst for others to reflect on their own choices.

A hush falls over the crowd as Elena's voice echoes through the barn, her heartfelt lyrics weaving a poignant narrative of yearning and resilience. It's a moment that transcends the art itself, reaching into the depths of every listener's soul. As the final note lingers in the air, it's as if the town collectively exhales, releasing years of suppressed dreams and unspoken desires.

But just as the applause begins to swell, a figure steps forward from the shadows—Elena's father, the mayor. His presence sends a ripple of uncertainty through the audience. Known for his traditional views, his reaction is eagerly anticipated. The room holds its breath, expecting either condemnation or acceptance.

In a surprising turn, the mayor pauses, surveying the transformed barn with a contemplative expression. Slowly, he begins to speak, his voice steady yet filled with emotion. He acknowledges the courage it takes to challenge the status quo and praises his daughter for her bravery in sharing her true self. His words are unexpected, yet sincere, and they mark a pivotal shift for the town.

The mayor's unexpected endorsement of the evening's events serves as a bridge between the old and the new, signaling a willingness to embrace change and support the evolving identities of the younger generation. It's a climactic moment that unites the community, breaking down barriers and fostering a newfound sense of unity.

As the night unfolds, conversations buzz with renewed energy. People who once clung to tradition now find themselves inspired by the evening's revelations. Jonah's art and Elena's song become symbols of hope and empowerment, encouraging others to explore their own paths without fear of judgment.

In this shared moment of transformation, the town begins to reimagine itself, blending the richness of its heritage with the vibrant possibilities of the future. It's a testament to the power of authenticity and the profound impact that a few courageous voices can have on an entire community.

Resolution:

Ultimately, both characters realize that while societal norms heavily influence personal decisions, the pursuit of true happiness lies in embracing their authentic selves. Elena chooses to reject the pressures of her predetermined path, instead pursuing a life that balances her passion for art and her responsibilities. Jonah begins teaching art classes to inspire others in the community, fostering a new generation of artists who feel free to express themselves.

In the end, the town itself begins to transform, encouraging individuality and creativity, illustrating how personal decisions can inspire societal change. The story ends on a powerful note of self-acceptance and the importance of community support in personal journeys, showing that while norms can be influential, they do not have to define one's path.

The town, once steeped in tradition and resistant to change, gradually blossoms into a vibrant tapestry of diverse voices and talents. Elena's decision to pursue her passion for songwriting, despite the expectations placed upon her, becomes a beacon of hope for many. Her songs, now celebrated at local events and gatherings, echo through the streets, serving as a reminder that authenticity is not only possible but also celebrated.

Jonah, with his newfound role as a mentor and teacher, trans-forms the local art scene into a thriving hub of creativity. His classes become a sanctuary for budding artists, a place where imagination knows no bounds and every brushstroke tells a story. The barn, once an abandoned relic, is now a lively art studio and gallery, where exhibitions are held regularly, showcasing the talents of the community.

The ripple effect of Elena and Jonah's courage is seen in the faces of the townspeople, who now embrace a broader spectrum of self-expression. The once rigid boundaries of tradition soften, making room for a mosaic of identities and dreams. Festivals evolve to include diverse forms of art and music, celebrating the unique contributions of each individual.

As the years pass, the town flourishes, its identity enriched by the stories and dreams of its people. Elena and Jonah, having forged their own paths, continue to inspire and uplift those around them. They understand that the journey to self-acceptance is ongoing, and they walk it with a sense of purpose and joy, knowing that they have sparked a change that will echo through generations.

In their journey, they have learned that true belonging comes not from conforming to expectations, but from creating a space where everyone is free to be themselves. And in this newfound freedom, the town finds its strength, united in its diversity, and ready to face whatever the future holds with open hearts and open minds.

Chapter 6

OPENING STATEMENTS

The Court of Existence

In the dimly lit chamber of the Appeals Court of Life, the atmosphere was thick with solemnity, as if the very walls held the weight of a thousand whispered truths. At the center of this hallowed space, Judge Aurelia Morrow sat with an air of both authority and introspection. Draped in her robe, a rich tapestry of deep blues and purples, she appeared both as a guardian and a seeker of the divine. Her gavel, an unassuming yet powerful tool of justice, rested within her grasp, a reminder of her duty—to uphold the essence of existence itself.

Judge Morrow had learned long ago that the cases presented before her were far more than mere disputes; they were the very fabric of life's tapestry. Each appeal, each plea, represented a fragile thread woven together by the hopes, dreams, regrets, and aspirations of the souls who existed beyond the mahogany doors of her courtroom. Here, the stakes transcended earthly concerns; they danced upon the ethereal realms of purpose, identity, and meaning.

As she prepared for the day's proceedings, she reflected on the significance of the cases she had presided over. Each story rendered was a mosaic of human experience—a tale of a lost love seeking redemption, a question of purpose from a weary soul wandering through a haze of discontent, and the silent cries of those struggling to carve out their identities in a chaotic world. In this court, each verdict held the power to alter the course of a life and illuminate shadows cast by existential doubt.

The first case of the day was called, a young man named Jack, whose struggle with identity emerged from the depths of societal expectations. As Jack stepped forward, his shoulders hunched beneath the burden of uncertainty, Judge Morrow's gaze softened with compassion. She could sense the turmoil within him, the desperate search for a self that felt authentic in a world of masks and facades.

"Tell me, Jack," she began, her voice a gentle breeze in the tension-filled room. "What brings you to seek the court's counsel today?"

His voice trembled, a mixture of fear and determination. "Your Honor, I feel lost. I've worn so many masks, trying to be who others want me to be, that I've forgotten who I am. I want to discover my true self and find a purpose that belongs to me."

Judge Morrow nodded, understanding the gravity of his words. In a world craving conformity, the quest for individuality seemed both noble and terrifying. "Identity is a journey," she explained, her own path echoing his. "It thrives in the spaces where we allow ourselves to question, to explore, and sometimes even to falter. What do those questions lead you to seek?"

As Jack articulated his feelings, Judge Morrow felt the ambient echoes of countless souls who had come before him, each wrestling with the fundamental questions of existence. For her, each case was an opportunity to shine a light on the darker corners of human experience, to invite souls into the warmth of understanding, and to explore the layers that defined their lives.

She was aware that within the realm of purpose lay a myriad of stories waiting to be told—stories of hope and despair, of acceptance and rejection. In this chamber, she was not just a judge but a witness to the human condition. Each verdict she issued was a note in the grand symphony of existence, playing a melody of empathy and shared experience.

As the session continued, Judge Morrow pondered the delicate threads connecting purpose and identity. These themes were not only the substance of the cases she reviewed but also the essence of her own life. Each interaction, each revelation, built a bridge toward greater understanding—not solely for those who stood before her but also for herself.

In the Court of Existence, every day was a new opportunity to sift through the ashes of discontent and ignite the flames of purpose. As the gavel struck, echoing through the chamber, she found herself at the intersection of authority and compassion, ever determined to illuminate the paths of those who sought clarity amidst the profound mysteries of life.

The day's proceedings unfolded like chapters in an ongoing epic, each case a verse in the endless poem of life. The next petitioner was an elderly woman named Eleanor, her eyes carrying the wisdom of years and the gentle sorrow of unspoken regrets. She approached with a quiet grace, the room holding its breath in anticipation of her story.

"Your Honor," Eleanor began, her voice a soft melody of resilience. "I've lived a long life, filled with love and loss, joy and sorrow. Yet, as I stand here, I wonder if I have left any meaningful mark on the world. Have my choices resonated beyond my own existence?"

Judge Morrow leaned forward, her gaze fixed intently on Eleanor. She understood the universal yearning for legacy, the desire to know that one's life had purpose and impact. "Eleanor," she replied, her voice imbued with warmth, "the imprints of our lives are often etched in the hearts of those we've touched, in ways both seen and unseen. Tell me about the moments that have shaped your journey."

As Eleanor recounted her tales of nurturing a family, of friendships forged and nurtured, and of kindnesses extended in times of need, the courtroom seemed to pulse with the collective heartbeat of shared humanity. Judge Morrow listened, her presence a balm to Eleanor's reflective soul.

In the Court of Existence, the narratives shared were revered as sacred threads in the tapestry of life. Each case brought forth a unique hue, weaving a picture of the human spirit's resilience and vulnerability. Judge Morrow knew that her role was not only to adjudicate but also to honor these stories, to offer solace and validation to those who bore the weight of existential quandaries.

As the day ended, the chamber echoed with the whispers of lives examined and understood. Judge Morrow rose, a quiet strength guiding her actions, aware that tomorrow would bring new stories and new souls seeking clarity. The Court of Existence stood as a testament to the enduring pursuit of meaning, where every gavel strike was a promise to hold space for the complexities of being.

Chapter 7
CASE FILES

The Trials We Face

Overview:

In "Case Files: The Trials We Face," we embark on a compelling journey through a series of unique legal narratives that encapsulate the essence of human experience. Each case file dives deep into the complexities of life, highlighting a diverse array of characters, each navigating their personal tribulations and triumphs. From the heart-wrenching moments of love and loss to the exhilarating highs of success and the crushing lows of failure, these stories are a testament to the resilience of the human spirit.

Through these narratives, readers are invited to ponder the intricate layers of justice and morality, as well as the enduring quest for truth and redemption. Each case, while distinct in its circumstances, shares a common thread—the profound impact of choices made, and paths taken. The stories unfold in courtrooms that become arenas for personal reckonings, where emotions run high and the stakes are undeniably real.

As we delve into the lives of Emily, Miguel, Sarah, and Jason, we encounter the universal themes of friendship, artistic aspiration, familial duty, and the relentless pursuit of justice. Their journeys not only reveal the legal challenges they face but also highlight the inner battles that shape their identities and destinies. In "Case Files: The Trials We Face," the courtroom is more than a place of judgment; it is a crucible where characters are tested and transformed, inviting readers to reflect on their own trials and triumphs.

Case 1: The Weight of Regret

Characters: Emily, the Plaintiff; Tom, the Defendant

Emily sues her childhood friend Tom for emotional distress after an unexpected betrayal leads to the unraveling of their long-standing friendship. As they recount the pivotal moments in their lives—shared dreams, whispered secrets, and eventual heartbreak—the courtroom becomes a stage for love lost and the weight of regret. Will Emily find closure, or will both characters be forever haunted by their past choices?

In the hushed solemnity of the courtroom, Emily and Tom sat on opposite sides, each enveloped in a world of reflection and remorse. Their eyes occasionally met, flickering with a mix of nostalgia and sorrow, as the echoes of laughter and promises from simpler times reverberated in their minds. The judge, with a keen understanding of the human heart, allowed the proceedings to unfold like a delicate dance—each argument and rebuttal a step toward understanding the intricacies of their fractured bond.

Emily, with a voice trembling yet resolute, recounted the moment when trust shattered like glass. The betrayal had been swift, a harsh jolt that left her reeling in disbelief. But beneath her composed exterior lay an ocean of longing for the friendship they once cherished. As she spoke, her words painted a vivid portrait of their shared history, each memory a brushstroke on the canvas of their intertwined lives.

Tom, in his defense, struggled to convey the complexity of his actions. His gaze was steady, yet his heart was heavy with the knowledge of the pain he had caused. It was a story of missteps and misunderstood intentions, a reminder that paths diverge and choices, once made, cast long shadows. His voice, tinged with regret, sought forgiveness not only from Emily but also from himself.

The courtroom murmured with empathy as witnesses—a tapestry of friends and family—shared their perspectives, weaving a narrative rich with insight and reflection. Each testimony revealed layers of the past, a mosaic of moments that shaped their relationship and brought them to this pivotal juncture.

As the trial ended, Emily and Tom faced the truth—a realization that healing was not found in victory or defeat, but in the courage to confront their past and the possibility of forgiveness. The verdict, though significant, paled in comparison to the greater resolution they sought: peace with their choices and a path forward, whether together or apart.

In "The Weight of Regret," the courtroom transcends its role as a mere arena for legal judgment, becoming a sanctuary for the heart. It reminds us of all that while we cannot change the past, we can choose how it defines us, embracing the lessons it imparts and the strength it demands.

Case 2: Dreams Deferred

Characters: Miguel, the Plaintiff; The City Council, the Defendants

Miguel, a passionate artist, takes his fight to the courtroom against the city council for unjustly denying his mural proposal aimed at revitalizing his neighborhood. Through the eyes of a community yearning for recognition, the case becomes a literary canvas that explores themes of identity, belonging, and the pursuit of dreams. Can Miguel's vision transform the community, or will bureaucracy stifle his artistic spirit?

In the heart of the city, where vibrant cultures intertwined and stories lingered in every corner, Miguel stood as a beacon of creativity and hope. His mural was more than art; it was a vision of unity, a tapestry of colors and shapes that spoke to the soul of the community. Yet, his dream was met with resistance, a bureaucratic wall that threatened to mute his vibrant palette.

The courtroom buzzed with anticipation as Miguel, with determination etched on his face, presented his case. His voice was rich with passion as he described the mural—a sprawling masterpiece that captured the essence of his neighborhood's spirit. Each brushstroke was a tribute to the people who called this place home, their struggles and triumphs immortalized in vivid hues.

The city council, seated across the aisle, maintained their stance, citing regulations and concerns. Their arguments, though grounded in policy, felt disconnected from the heartbeat of the community. It was a clash between the sterile language of legislation and the raw, emotive power of art.

As witnesses took the stand, a mosaic of voices emerged. Neighbors, artists, and local leaders shared their stories, painting a picture of a community eager for change. They spoke of neglected streets and forgotten spaces, yearning for revitalization and recognition. Miguel's mural was not just art; it was a symbol of hope, a beacon for future generations.

Miguel listened intently, his heart swelling with pride and responsibility. This was more than a personal battle; it was a collective dream. He knew that art had the power to heal, to inspire, and to bring people together. His fight was not just for a mural, but for the soul of his community.

As the trial unfolded, the courtroom became a theater of dreams deferred and aspirations reignited. The judge, with a sense of fairness and an ear for truth, weighed the arguments with care. In the end, the decision would reflect not only the letter of the law but the spirit of a community longing for transformation.

In "Dreams Deferred," the courtroom becomes a stage for a narrative as old as time—the struggle between innovation and tradition, between the status quo and the desire for change. As Miguel stands at the crossroads of his artistic journey, his story reminds us of the power of perseverance and the enduring belief that dreams, no matter how deferred, are worth fighting for.

Case 3: The Burden of Legacy

Characters: Sarah, the Plaintiff; The Estate of Her Father, the Defendant

In a legal battle over her late father's estate, Sarah contends with the shadows of familial expectations and unresolved grievances. The trial unearths painful memories of their relationship and the legacy he left behind—a fortune entwined with secrets. As Sarah confronts the truths of her father's life, can she redefine her own identity or will she become a prisoner of her inheritance?

The courtroom buzzed with a solemn intensity as Sarah took the stand, her heart a tempest of emotions. She was a daughter seeking more than just material inheritance; she was searching for understanding, for closure, and a sense of belonging that had eluded her since her father's passing.

Her father's legacy was one of remarkable success, a towering figure in the business world whose decisions had ripple effects far beyond their family. Yet, beneath the public image lay a tapestry of complex relationships, unspoken expectations, and a vault of secrets that Sarah was determined to unlock. The estate, rich in assets yet fraught with tension, was the backdrop for a deeper, more personal struggle.

As the trial unfolded, Sarah's composure was both her armor and her burden. She recounted moments from her childhood, snapshots of a life shadowed by her father's ambitions. Her voice, though steady, carried the weight of years spent in the shadow of a man whose love was often eclipsed by his own aspirations.

The opposing counsel, representing the estate, presented a meticulous case, highlighting the intricate web of legalities surrounding her father's wealth. Yet, they could not suppress the emotional gravity of the proceedings—a daughter grappling with the duality of love and resentment, of admiration and disappointment.

Family members and confidants were called to testify, each adding a piece to the puzzle of Sarah's past. Their stories painted a portrait of a man both revered and misunderstood, his legacy a mosaic of triumphs and regrets. They spoke of a father who, while absent at times, had also left indelible marks on those around him.

Sarah listened, her resolve unwavering, yet each testimony chipped away at the barriers she had built. This was more than a fight for financial inheritance; it was a quest for personal liberation, a chance to step out from the shadows and into her own light.

The judge, tasked with untangling the legal from the emotional, approached the case with empathy and fairness. The decision would shape Sarah's future, but the journey itself was transforming her, offering a path to understanding and reconciliation with her father's memory.

In "The Burden of Legacy," the courtroom morphs into a crucible for Sarah's self-discovery. It is a reminder that inheritance is not merely the wealth we receive, but the lessons and legacies we choose to embrace or redefine. Through her struggle, Sarah learns that true legacy lies in the courage to forge her own path, honoring her father's memory while claiming her own identity.

Case 4: Redemption and Reconciliation

Characters: Jason, the Defendant; Lisa, the Plaintiff

After serving time for a crime he didn't commit, Jason seeks compensation from the state. Lisa, the prosecutor during his trial, now grapples with her own conscience as she discovers the truth behind the wrongful conviction. Their paths collide in a courtroom filled with tension and moral dilemmas, as both characters seek personal redemption and a chance for reconciliation. Can justice truly be served, or is it always an illusion?

The courtroom was heavy with anticipation, a silent witness to the unfolding drama between two individuals whose lives had been inexorably altered by the past. Jason stood tall, his demeanor a mixture of quiet strength and the scars of an unjust ordeal. His eyes, once filled with anger and bitterness, now held a spark of hope—a desire for justice not only in the eyes of the law but in the depths of his soul.

Lisa, once a steadfast prosecutor, now found herself on the other side of the moral divide. The weight of her role in Jason's conviction sat heavily on her shoulders, a reminder of the fallibility inherent in the pursuit of justice. Her journey towards understanding had been long and fraught with self-reflection, a quest to right the wrongs of her past actions.

As the case unfolded, the courtroom became a tapestry of conflicting emotions and revelations. Jason's defense team presented irrefutable evidence of his innocence, each piece dismantling the case that had once condemned him. Witness testimonies painted a picture of a man wronged by the system, his life derailed by an injustice. Through it all, Jason remained dignified, a testament to the resilience of the human spirit.

Lisa, faced with the undeniable truth, took the stand with a heavy heart. Her voice, though steady, carried the tremors of regret and the earnestness of someone seeking redemption. She spoke of the pressure to secure convictions, the blind spots that had clouded her judgment, and the newfound understanding that had led her to this moment. Her testimony was both an apology to Jason and a plea for forgiveness from herself.

The courtroom murmured with a mix of empathy and tension, the gravity of the situation palpable in every corner. As the judge deliberated, the air was thick with anticipation, each heartbeat echoing the desire for a just outcome.

In the end, the verdict was a triumph for truth—a recognition of Jason's innocence and a step toward healing. Yet, beyond the legal resolution lay the deeper, more personal journey of reconciliation. Jason and Lisa, once adversaries, now stood on the cusp of understanding, their paths converging in a shared acknowledgment of the past and a hopeful gaze toward the future.

"Redemption and Reconciliation" serves as a poignant reminder that justice is not merely a destination, but a journey marked by introspection, courage, and the willingness to forgive. As Jason and Lisa navigate the complexities of their newfound paths, they illuminate the enduring truth that redemption is possible, and reconciliation, while challenging, can lead to profound transformation.

Conclusion:

In the end, "Case Files: The Trials We Face" is more than a mere collection of legal dramas; it is a tapestry of human perseverance, woven with threads of empathy, resilience, and the indomitable spirit of those who dare to dream of a better world. As readers journey through these stories, they are invited to ponder the profound questions that linger in the spaces between right and wrong, and to embrace the timeless truth that while the path to justice may be fraught with challenges, it is also paved with opportunities for growth, understanding, and redemption.

Chapter 8

WITNESS TESTIMONIES

Perspectives on Truth

Family Testimony: The Echo of Childhood

Mom: "When I think back to those days, I remember your laughter echoing through the halls. You'd run into the living room, arms outstretched, always looking for approval. But do you remember the time you fell off your bike, scraped your knees, and cried? You didn't just cry because of the pain; you cried because you thought you had disappointed us. That moment shaped you; it taught you that failure wasn't just a bruise but a source of fear. Seeing it that way made you so much more cautious later. It's a memory tinged with the sweetness of innocence lost."

Dad: "I saw strength in you that I believed could carry you through anything. I remember when you stood up to that kid in school. You were terrified, but you faced him, and that was a decisive moment. You learned that sometimes standing up means more than just physical bravery; it's about defending what you believe in, even when it feels like you're losing."

Each of these memories paints a vivid picture of your childhood, offering a glimpse into the experiences that have molded you. Your mom's recollection reveals your sensitivity and the early seeds of self-perception, where a simple fall became a lesson in vulnerability. Meanwhile, your dad's memory highlights a different facet of your character—your courage and the values you held close, even in the face of fear.

These familial reflections underscore the duality of your growth: the interplay between fear and bravery, caution and conviction. They remind you that each moment, whether seen as a stumble or a triumph, contributed to the person you are today. It's a testament to how the echoes of childhood resonate, shaping your journey with layers of love, challenge, and understanding.

As you weave these memories into your narrative, remember that both the shadows and the light are integral to your story. They are the threads that, when combined, create a rich tapestry of who you've become and who you continue to be.

Friend Testimony: The Lens of Friendship

Sara: "I knew you at a time when you were still figuring out who you were. To me, you were this vibrant person, always searching for the next adventure. But I didn't see the struggles you kept hidden. When you told me about the anxiety that overwhelmed you during those late high school days, I had no idea it made you question your worth. To me, you had it all—talent, charm, everything. Funny how our perspectives differ, isn't it? Yours felt like a shadow; mine was bright, too bright."

Josh: "Looking back on our friendship, I see how different our realities were. You often praised me for my confidence in the classroom, but I always felt like a fraud. We each wore masks, hiding our internal battles. The truth is, your laughter was often a façade to cover your heartbreak, just as mine was. It's funny how we both believed we were alone, yet we were fighting side by side with a kind of empathy neither of us fully understood."

These reflections from friends offer a poignant glimpse into the complexities of friendship and self-perception. Sara's and Josh's testimonies highlight how we often see in others the strengths we feel we lack in ourselves, creating a mirror of admiration and misunderstanding. This mirroring effect underscores the duality of perception; while Sara saw only vibrancy, the protagonist battled unseen shadows. Similarly, Josh's recognition of their shared masks reveals a silent camaraderie where vulnerability was both a weakness and a bond.

These insights invite a deeper understanding of how friendships enrich and challenge our narratives. They illuminate the idea that friendship is not just about shared experiences but also about the silent battles we endure together, often unknowingly. Through these testimonies, the protagonist learns that the connections formed during those formative years were woven from both shared laughter and hidden heartaches, each thread adding texture to their personal tapestry.

As these memories are interwoven with those from family and mentors, they create a richer, more nuanced picture of the protagonist's journey. The interplay of differing perspectives—each with its unique shade of truth—encourages the protagonist to embrace the complexity of their story, understanding that it is the sum of many voices, each contributing to the beautiful mosaic of their life.

Mentor Testimony: Guidance and Insight

Mr. Thompson: "In my eyes, you always showed potential. But potential is just a starting line; it's the choices you make that define your path. I remember the first time you hesitated to speak up in class. You felt your voice didn't matter. I saw truth in that—a truth wrapped in self-doubt and fear—yet in those moments, I also saw the spark of someone who would eventually find their voice. My perspective as your teacher was partially flawed. I assumed your silence meant apathy when it was the weight of your thoughts. The truth is complex; it's woven from countless viewpoints."

Mr. Thompson's reflection highlights a pivotal aspect of growth: the journey from silence to voice. His words underscore the importance of recognizing the power in one's own voice, even when it feels muted by self-doubt. Through his guidance, the protagonist learns that silence does not equate to absence of thought or feeling. Instead, it is often the precursor to finding and embracing one's true voice.

Ms. Rivera:

"You were always more insightful than you gave yourself credit for. I watched you wrestle with ideas that others might have dismissed easily. Your depth of thought was your strength, even when it felt like a burden. Remember the project on societal change? You hesitated, unsure if your ideas were worth sharing, but when you did, it was transformative. You saw layers and nuances that others missed, and that's a rare gift. Our discussions taught me as much as they taught you. It's a reminder that learning is a two-way street; you have as much to offer as you must learn."

These mentor insights provide a lens through which the protagonist can appreciate their own growth. Mr. Thompson's and Ms. Rivera's experiences with the protagonist reveal the tension between internal doubt and external perception, illustrating how mentors can see potential where individuals might only see hesitation. They encourage the protagonist to recognize the value in their unique perspective and the impact it can have when shared with the world.

As these narratives blend with those from family and friends, they contribute to a multifaceted view of the protagonist's journey. Each perspective, whether familial, friendly, or educational, adds depth and understanding to the tapestry of their life, highlighting the intricate interplay of encouragement, self-discovery, and the gradual embrace of one's own voice. In this collaborative narrative, the protagonist learns that growth is both a personal and shared experience, nurtured by the insights and support of those who walk alongside them.

The Subjectivity of Truth:

These testimonies serve to illuminate a profound theme: truth is neither singular nor immutable. Each voice carries a unique perspective that informs the protagonist's understanding of themself, often conflicting and reshaping the narrative they live. The truth of a memory, such as how a childhood bike accident is perceived, differs drastically depending on the witness and their own experiences.

The protagonist might see their past as a series of failures in the shadows, while others illuminate moments of bravery or warmth. The challenge lies in reconciling these differing truths and forming an authentic narrative from them all.

In navigating their truths, the protagonist learns that the journey is not about finding a singular truth but embracing the myriad ways life can be perceived, reshaping their own story in the process. Each voice adds complexity, revealing that understanding oneself is a tapestry woven from the varied threads of experience, perception, and emotion. Thus, the protagonist's ultimate realization is that their life story isn't solely theirs; it's a collaborative tapestry rich with diverse viewpoints, each contributing to the tapestry that is their existence.

This realization fosters a deeper sense of empathy and connection with those around them, as they come to appreciate the beauty in diversity of thought and experience. It encourages them to listen more intently, to seek out the stories and perspectives of others, and to understand that every interaction holds the potential for growth and learning.

In embracing this multifaceted truth, the protagonist finds freedom. They are no longer bound by a single narrative or a rigid self-concept. Instead, they become an ever-evolving being, open to change and new interpretations. This openness allows them to live more fully, with a heart and mind ready to absorb the richness of the world around them.

As they continue their journey, they carry with them the wisdom that life's meaning is not fixed but is continually crafted through the interplay of experiences. They learn to cherish each moment, each relationship, and each story as an integral part of their on-going evolution, understanding that every thread, no matter how delicate or bold, contributes to the beautiful tapestry of their life.

Chapter 9

EVIDENCE PRESENTED

The Choices We Make

Choices of Consequence

Character Introduction: The Prosecutor of Regret

As the courtroom doors creaked open, a woman stepped forward, her presence commanding, yet cloaked in an aura of melancholic wisdom. Her name was Eleanor Graves, the embodiment of regret, with eyes that shimmered like glassy stones, worn smooth by the tide of time. A former prodigy in the legal world, now a seasoned prosecutor, Eleanor was fueled by a burning need to confront others with their choices—especially those she had failed to confront during her own bygone era.

Eleanor had seen countless lives altered by decisions made in fleeting moments. She believed that every choice bore weight—some light and inconsequential, others heavy as a heart full of sorrow. Her own life echoed with the reverberations of what-ifs: an abandoned dream of practicing criminal law to serve justice, a relationship left untended, and opportunities overlooked—all of which now festered as an intricate mosaic of regret.

In her latest case, she was pitted against a young man named Jake Wilkins, a former classmate whose bright future had been derailed by a series of impulsive decisions—a drug-fueled night leading to a tragic accident that claimed the life of an innocent woman. Jake stood at the center of this intense trial, wrestling with both his guilt and a burgeoning desire for redemption.

Eleanor saw in Jake not just a defendant, but a reflection of her own past—a reminder of the choices that had once defined her. Each step she took into the courtroom was a step into her own history, a journey through the shadows of her own decisions.

Yet, she was determined to use her understanding of regret to guide others toward redemption, hoping that by illuminating the impact of choices, she might help them escape the same pitfalls that had ensnared her.

As the trial commenced, Eleanor's approach was not merely about prosecuting Jake for his actions but about fostering a deeper understanding of accountability. She believed in holding a mirror up to Jake, allowing him to see the full spectrum of his decisions—not to condemn him, but to offer a path toward healing. Her questions were precise, designed to peel back the layers of his choices, to reveal the humanity beneath the guilt.

Throughout the proceedings, Eleanor's empathy became her greatest tool. She spoke not just to the jury, but to Jake directly, intertwining her own stories of missed chances and resilience with the evidence at hand. Her goal was not just to secure a verdict, but to provoke introspection and growth, both in Jake and in herself.

In this intricate dance between past mistakes and future possibilities, Eleanor and Jake found themselves entangled in a shared narrative—a narrative that transcended the confines of the courtroom. It was a tale of redemption, of confronting the demons of one's past, and of striving to craft a future not dictated by regret but inspired by the lessons learned from it.

Setting the Scene: Confronting the Past

As the trial began, Eleanor stood before the jury, an embodiment of the harsh reality that choices would forever alter the course of one's life. "Ladies and gentlemen of the jury," she began, her voice steady yet infused with emotion, "we are here today not just to seek justice for the life lost but to explore the labyrinth of choices that led us down this dark path."

With each piece of evidence laid bare before the court—text messages, CCTV footage, and testimonies from witnesses—Eleanor meticulously painted a picture of that fateful night. Each choice Jake made, each reckless decision to join his friends in an innocent celebration of freedom, was dissected, revealing the trajectory that spiraled out of control.

As Jake listened, he felt the weight of his past choices pressing down like a heavy cloak of guilt. While he had sought solace in his friends, his decisions had irrevocably altered the lives of many, including his own. Eleanor's voice became a haunting echo, reminding not just Jake but everyone present of the fragility of life influenced by inconsequential choices.

The courtroom held its breath, the air thick with the gravity of the moment. Eleanor's words resonated with an urgency that transcended the mere facts of the case, touching on the universal human experience of choice and consequence. She moved with a deliberate grace, her presence commanding attention as she wove the narrative of that fateful night, each detail a thread in the complex tapestry of human error and regret.

Amidst the silent contemplation of the jury, Eleanor paused, allowing the weight of her words to settle. Her gaze swept the room, landing momentarily on Jake, who sat with his head bowed, a young man grappling with the enormity of his actions. Her heart ached with a familiar pang of empathy, for she understood all too well the burden of choices left unexamined.

"Choices," she continued, "are the building blocks of our lives. They define who we are, but they do not have to confine us. This is a story not only of loss but of potential rebirth. It is a chance for all of us to reflect on the paths we have taken and the paths we might yet forge."

Eleanor's voice softened, a hint of hope threading through the somber narrative. She knew that this trial was more than a legal battle; it was an opportunity for transformation—for Jake, for herself, and perhaps for every soul present in that room. In her heart, she held the belief that even amidst the darkest moments, the seeds of redemption could be sown, nurtured by the lessons of the past.

As the proceedings continued, Eleanor remained steadfast in her pursuit of justice, yet her vision transcended mere retribution. She aimed to illuminate the power of self-awareness, the courage of owning one's actions, and the possibility of change. Her dedication to these ideals, forged in the crucible of her own regrets, became a beacon for Jake, guiding him toward a future where his past need not dictate his destiny.

In this shared journey of introspection and accountability, Eleanor and Jake stood at the crossroads of their lives, poised to embrace the uncertain future with renewed purpose and an understanding that every choice, no matter how small, carries the potential to reshape one's world.

The Confrontation: The Weight of Regret

During a pivotal moment in the trial, Eleanor chose to confront Jake directly. "What would you say to the family of the victim?" she asked, her piercing gaze locking onto him. "What can you say that would make any difference?"

Jake, once brimming with bravado, was now stripped of his defenses. He stammered, "I...I didn't mean for any of this to happen. I wish I had made different choices."

Eleanor took a step closer, her voice softening just slightly. "But you did make those choices, didn't you? And each of them led you here, to this courtroom, to this reckoning. We all write our own stories, but it's the consequences of our choices that carve out our ending."

In that moment, as he stared into the depths of her eyes, Jake was forced to confront not just the weight of his decisions, but the haunting reality that everyone, including Eleanor, was a mosaic of their past—each cracked piece telling a story of missed opportunities and deep regrets.

The courtroom was silent, the air thick with the shared understanding of life's complexities. Eleanor paused, her words hanging like a delicate thread, connecting the disparate pieces of their shared humanity. She knew that this moment was not just about judgment but about the possibility of redemption.

"Regret," Eleanor continued, her voice a gentle echo in the stillness, "is a powerful teacher. It reminds us of our fallibility, yet it also offers us a chance to grow, to change, and to seek forgiveness—not just from others, but from ourselves."

Jake nodded slowly, his eyes brimming with unshed tears. For the first time, he saw the path before him not as a dead end but as a crossroads. In Eleanor, he saw a guide who understood the terrain of regret and the potential for transformation that lay beyond it.

"We can't change the past," Eleanor said, "but we can choose how it shapes us. We can choose to learn from it, to honor the lives it has touched, and to forge a future illuminated by the light of understanding and compassion."

The jurors, witnesses, and everyone present felt the profound impact of Eleanor's words. It was a call to introspection, a reminder that while choices carry weight, so too does the potential for healing and renewal.

As the trial continued, this moment of confrontation became a turning point—not only for Jake but for Eleanor as well. She found herself reflecting on her own choices, feeling the gentle release of long-held burdens as she watched Jake take his first steps toward a future not defined by his past mistakes but by the lessons he'd learned.

In the quiet aftermath of that pivotal exchange, the courtroom transformed from a place of judgment into a space of possibility, where the past was acknowledged, and the future awaited, ready to be written anew.

Conclusion: Embracing Consequence for Growth

As the trial unfolded, Eleanor's challenge to Jake—and to her-self—was not merely about laying blame or seeking punishment. It became an examination of how we grow from our past. Jake learned to embrace his history, albeit painful, and place it along-side his desire for redemption, while Eleanor was reminded that her own choices had shaped her path in unforeseen ways.

In this poignant exploration of choices and their consequences, both characters embarked on journeys toward understand-ing—Eleanor learning to let go of her burdens of regret, and Jake striving to embrace his mistakes, working to carve a future de-fined by mindful decisions rather than past missteps. As the trial ended, it became clear that the choices we make, painful as they may seem, can lead us to the very truths we need to face—about ourselves and the lives we lead.

Through the tension and turmoil, a profound transformation took place. Eleanor and Jake, once strangers on opposite sides of the courtroom, found themselves united by a shared understand-ing. The air was charged with a sense of resolution as the final verdict approached.

The jury deliberated, aware that their decision would not only affect Jake but would also serve as a testament to the power of change and redemption. When they returned, the atmosphere was thick with anticipation. Eleanor stood tall, her heart steady, knowing that regardless of the outcome, the trial had already fulfilled a deeper purpose.

In the end, Jake was held accountable for his actions, yet the sentencing emphasized rehabilitation over retribution. It was a chance for him to rebuild, to atone for his mistakes by contributing positively to society. Eleanor watched as Jake accepted his future with a newfound determination, his path illuminated by the lessons of the past.

As the courtroom emptied, Eleanor lingered, reflecting on the journey she had been a part of. Her role as a prosecutor had always been to seek justice, but this case had taught her that justice could be a pathway to healing, not just for the victims and their families but for the defendants and herself as well.

Walking out into the crisp evening air, Eleanor felt the weight of her own regrets lift slightly. She realized that like Jake, she too had the power to redefine her story—not by erasing the past, but by building upon it with compassion and wisdom.

The trial had concluded, yet the echoes of its lessons would resonate long after. For Eleanor, for Jake, and for all who had witnessed the proceedings, it was a reminder that while the choices we make can cast long shadows, they also have the power to illuminate the way forward.

Chapter 10

THE JURY OF SELF

Judgment and Reflection

In the quiet hum of their thoughts, the main character stands before an invisible jury, composed not of peers or elders, but of their own self-judgment. This internal tribunal comes alive whenever they are confronted with stories—be it from friends, family, or even strangers—about lives lived, choices made, and paths taken. Each narrative they encounter becomes a mirror, reflecting not only the lives of others but also the complexities of their own existence.

As they listen to tales of triumph and despair, the character grapples with an ever-present dichotomy: the societal standards of success and the fierce individuality that defines personal fulfillment. Society lays out a roadmap, often marked by wealth, prestige, or visible achievement, but these landmarks clash with the nuanced realities of human experience. It is in this tension that the character experiences their internal conflict—a push and pull between what they've been taught to value externally and what resonates within.

The first case presented to the jury is of a high-achieving acquaintance, whose success is adorned with accolades and financial security. The character feels the immediate impact of societal approval wash over them—a powerful force that compels admiration but also ignites a sense of inadequacy. Is success merely a collection of trophies, or can it exist in forms that are less visible, in the quiet satisfaction of a life well-lived but not glamorous? They ponder the sacrifices made in pursuit of this acclaim and start to question whether the journey taken was worth the personal losses incurred along the way.

Next, the jury turns to the story of a friend who opted for a less conventional life, choosing passion over profit, yet struggling to make ends meet. This narrative stirs a wave of empathy within the character. Here lies a kindred spirit, someone who defied the societal mold and ventured into the unknown, yet whose struggles paint a picture of a life lived on the fringes of success. The character reflects on their upbringing, where deviation from the conventional path was often met with skepticism. Could it be that true courage lies in choosing authenticity over acceptance? The character's self-judgment becomes a battleground, wrestling with fear and longing, acceptance, and regret.

As they sift through the experiences presented, a deeper reality emerges: the societal expectations that shape perceptions of success and failure are often arbitrary and superficial, yet they hold a tremendous weight in the character's mind. The internal jury deliberates—how do they measure themselves against these narratives? Is their own pursuit of happiness valid when it doesn't align with conventional standards?

In this process of reflection, the character recognizes that self-judgment is both a destructive force and a catalyst for growth. It pushes them to evaluate their choices and consider their values while simultaneously creating a paralyzing environment of self-doubt and comparison. They realize that to find peace, they must redefine success on their own terms, acknowledging that each life is unique and deserving of respect, regardless of its outward appearance.

With newfound clarity, the character stands up to the jury of self, framing the argument for their worth not in the light of what society deems admirable but through a lens of authentic existence. They understand that success is subjective, entwined with personal values, aspirations, and circumstances. As their internal conflict gives way to acceptance, they embrace the complexity of their journey, enriched by the lives of others without being overshadowed by them.

In the end, the character learns that the most profound judgment comes not from external comparisons but from embracing their own narrative, with all its imperfections and triumphs. By doing so, they dismantle the societal chains that bound their perceptions and, in turn, grant themselves the freedom to live unencumbered by the weight of judgment—an invaluable lesson in the ongoing journey of self-discovery.

They realize that life is not a competition but a personal exploration of meaning and fulfillment. This understanding allows them to approach each day with gratitude and curiosity, rather than anxiety and self-reproach. They come to see that every path, no matter how winding or unconventional, has its own beauty and worth.

The character embraces the notion that life is a tapestry of experiences, each thread contributing to the richness of the whole. They find peace in knowing that their journey is uniquely theirs and that their worth is inherent, not dictated by external validation or societal norms.

With this newfound perspective, they navigate their world with a sense of empowerment and joy, ready to face new challenges and celebrate their own distinct narrative. The internal jury becomes less of a tribunal and more of a council, guiding them with wisdom and compassion rather than judgment and fear.

The character discovers that true liberation lies in the acceptance of oneself—and in that acceptance, they find the courage to live authentically and wholeheartedly.

Chapter 11

THE VERDICT

Acceptance and Forgiveness

"The law is the embodiment of the moral sentiment of the people."
—William Blackstone

As our narrative progresses, we witness profound transformations as characters grapple with their pasts and emerge into a realm of acceptance and forgiveness.

One character, burdened by guilt from a long-ago mistake, initially seeks retribution against those they perceive to have wronged them. However, as the story advances, interactions with a kind-hearted mentor guide them to reflect deeply on their choices. Through these conversations, they begin to realize that holding onto resentment only shackles them to their past. In a pivotal moment, they take a brave step toward reconciling with those they have hurt. This act not only liberates the other party but also allows the character to start forgiving themselves, illustrating how acceptance can lead to personal freedom.

As they navigate this journey, the character discovers that forgiveness is not a single act but a continuous process. Their mentor, a wise and compassionate figure, shares stories of their own struggles with forgiveness, offering insights that resonate deeply. These stories become a source of inspiration, revealing that acceptance goes hand in hand with self-compassion.

Gradually, the character begins to see the world through a lens of empathy, understanding that everyone carries their own burdens. This newfound perspective fosters a sense of connection with others, breaking down barriers that once seemed insurmountable. They start to engage in meaningful dialogue with those they have wronged, listening with an open heart and offering sincere apologies.

This transformation is mirrored in the way they carry themselves—lighter and more at peace. They find joy in small acts of kindness and begin to cultivate relationships built on trust and mutual respect. Through this journey, they learn that true forgiveness is an act of courage, one that requires vulnerability and the willingness to let go of the past.

Their story serves as a powerful reminder that while the path to acceptance and forgiveness may be challenging, it is also immensely rewarding. By embracing their imperfections and making amends, they pave the way for a future filled with hope and possibility.

Another character, once bitter and isolated due to past grievances, gradually opens their heart to the possibility of connection. Initially unwilling to forgive those who betrayed them, they are challenged by an unexpected friendship formed with someone who mirrors their pain. This bond highlights the power of empathy, pushing them to confront their pain rather than dwell in it. As they slowly learn to let go of their grudges, they find solace in shared vulnerabilities, transforming their bitterness into compassion and understanding.

Their journey is marked by small yet significant milestones, each contributing to their evolving perspective on life and relationships. They begin to appreciate the beauty in shared experiences and the strength that comes from vulnerability. The friendship serves as a catalyst for change, encouraging them to reach out to others they had previously shut out.

As they navigate this new terrain of openness, they discover that extending forgiveness to others also means forgiving themselves. This realization propels them forward, allowing them to mend fractured connections and build new, healthier ones. The transformation is evident in their interactions, as they engage with others more sincerely and warmly, breaking down the barriers of isolation they had once built around themselves.

Through this process, they learn that forgiveness is a gift they give to themselves—a release from the chains of resentment that frees them to live more fully. The once-bitter character finds a renewed sense of purpose, driven by the understanding that empathy and compassion can bridge even the deepest divides.

In this newfound state of grace, they become a beacon of hope for others who struggle with similar challenges, proving that change is possible when one opens their heart to the healing power of connection and understanding. Their journey, like those of the other characters, underscores the profound truth that while the road to acceptance and forgiveness may be arduous, it leads to a life enriched by love and peace.

Furthermore, a third character faces a pivotal reconciliation with a family member after decades of estrangement. The confrontation between them is fraught with unresolved issues, heartache, and blame. Yet, through heartfelt dialogue and moments of vulnerability, they dismantle the walls they've constructed over the years. This journey towards forgiveness is not immediate; it requires patience, patience that pays off when they finally share a moment of mutual understanding. Their transformation embodies the idea that accepting the past does not erase the pain but empowers them to embrace a future free from its shackles.

In the aftermath of this emotional reunion, the two family members find themselves navigating a new relationship, one built on mutual respect and understanding. They begin to appreciate the moments they share, no longer shackled by the shadows of their past grievances. As they rebuild their bond, they discover shared interests and cherished memories that had been buried beneath years of silence.

This renewed connection creates a ripple effect, inspiring others within their family to seek reconciliation and healing. Family gatherings, once tense and fraught with unspoken tensions, gradually become occasions of joy and laughter. The courage displayed by these two characters serves as a beacon of hope for the entire family, illustrating that healing is possible when individuals choose to confront their pain with honesty and compassion.

Through their journey, they learn that forgiveness is a continuous act, a dance of understanding and empathy that requires both individuals to remain open and willing to grow together. Their story highlights the importance of communication in healing fractured relationships and shows that even the deepest wounds can begin to heal with time, patience, and love.

Their reconciliation becomes a testament to the power of human connection and the incredible resilience of the heart. It reinforces the notion that while the path to forgiveness and acceptance is often complex and challenging, it is also one of profound beauty and transformation.

In conclusion, "The Verdict: Acceptance and Forgiveness" skillfully illustrates that the path to healing is often winding and fraught with challenges. The characters' transformations demonstrate that true acceptance and forgiveness aren't about absolving others; they're equally about liberating oneself from the burden of the past. As they learn to reconcile with their histories, they foster a newfound hope, emphasizing that moving forward is possible when one dares to confront the ghosts of yesterday. This profound evolution serves as a testament to the resilience of the human spirit and the healing power of forgive-ness.

The narrative leaves us with a powerful message: no matter how deep the wounds or how long the silence, there is always room for growth and renewal. By bravely facing their pasts, the characters illuminate a path to redemption and peace not only for them-selves but also for those around them. Their journeys remind us that while the scars of our experiences may never fully disappear, they can become part of a tapestry of strength and wisdom. Through understanding, empathy, and the courage to forgive, we can build bridges where there were once walls, creating a world where love and compassion reign supreme.

Chapter 12

APPEAL FOR A NEW CHAPTER

Growth and Redemption

"Justice delayed is justice denied." —*William E. Gladstone*

As the towering walls of the courtroom faded behind her, Elena took a deep breath, the crisp air infused with the scent of impending rain. Each case she had presided over was imprinted on her soul—like ink on paper, indelible and transformative. The echoes of heart-wrenching testimonies and the weight of justice had sculpted her, carving out spaces for both empathy and resilience within her.

In her early days as a judge, the authority of her title had felt suffocating, enforcing a sense of detachment that kept her issues at bay. Yet, it was amidst the harrowing tales of loss and triumph that she began to uncover the fragments of her own story—stories of flawed humans navigating the labyrinth of their lives, much like her own. The defendant who'd found the courage to admit his failings; the victim who transformed bitterness into forgiveness. Every trial had not only tested their mettle but ignited a flicker of hope in her heart.

The lessons learned were blurred with tears and triumphs: the realization that everyone walks a path muddied by mistakes, that redemption is a tapestry woven through choices both small and monumental. In the courtroom, Elena saw reflections of herself—the fear of failure, the yearning for approval, and the struggle to let go of the past's grip. Now, as she stood on the precipice of a new chapter, she could finally allow herself to embrace the notion of change.

As she entered the small café across the street, the cozy warmth enveloped her. There, she spotted David—a fellow advocate and steadfast friend, a man who had feared his own shadows but emerged with the light of possibility in his eyes. Together, their conversations had evolved from discussions of legality to profound dialogues about second chances. Today, he would share his latest venture: a community outreach initiative aimed at supporting individuals reentering society after serving time.

"Elena," he greeted, his smile infectious. "Today's the day we plant seeds of hope."

The words resonated, and for the first time in a long while, Elena felt the weight of her past lift. They discussed dreams of renewal, where the mistakes of yesterday would pave the way for tomorrow's promise. Plans took shape, emerging from the ashes of their shared experiences, each idea vibrant with the potential of change.

In that moment, they both understood that growth is a continuance rather than a conclusion. The trials they had faced—both in and out of the courtroom—were not mere burdens but teachers guiding them toward resilience. Elena grasped the idea that hope does not belong solely to the innocent; it is a thread that can be rewoven by anyone willing to confront their choices, no matter how daunting.

As rain began to patter softly against the window, she felt an enveloping warmth—a promise of new beginnings, a story yet to be told. Together with David, she would amplify the voices longing to be heard, the souls yearning for redemption.

Elena leaned closer, her heart full of renewed purpose. The world outside was shifting, and so was she. With growth came the willingness to forgive, not just others, but herself. She understood then that every ending could lead to new beginnings, and with each turn of the page, a beautiful chapter awaited—one where hope clung steadfastly, and change was not just possible, but inevitable.

In that café, amidst laughter and dreams, Elena embraced the future—a testament to the belief that redemption blooms not just in the light of success, but in the journey of becoming.

She and David sat there, surrounded by the hum of conversation and the comforting aroma of freshly brewed coffee, sketching out the blueprint for their initiative. They envisioned a sanctuary where stories of redemption were celebrated, where learning from past missteps was encouraged, and where every individual was seen not for their mistakes, but for their potential to grow and contribute positively to their community.

The café was alive with a sense of purpose, as if it too understood the importance of the seeds being planted. Elena imagined the lives they might touch—people standing at their own crossroads, searching for guidance and understanding. She felt a deep connection to these future stories, knowing all too well the power of a single moment of grace.

As they finalized their plans, Elena and David knew the path ahead would not be without its challenges. But they were ready to walk it, hand in hand with those who sought to rebuild their lives. This was more than a project; it was a mission, a calling to make a difference, to offer a hand to those reaching up from darkness into light.

With each passing hour, the rain outside became a symphony, a reminder that even the heaviest storms eventually nourish the earth, bringing forth life anew. Elena's heart was full, her spirit buoyed by the knowledge that she was not alone in this journey. Together, they would forge a new narrative—one where compassion and understanding were the guiding stars.

As they left the café, the rain had slowed to a gentle drizzle, a cleansing rain that blessed their newfound resolve. Elena looked at David, their shared vision reflected in his eyes and felt a profound gratitude for the path that had led her here. She was ready to embrace whatever came next, confident in the knowledge that with each step forward, they were helping to write a story of hope and transformation for all who dared to dream of a second chance.

Chapter 13

THE FINAL RULINGS

Legacy and Impact

As we reach the conclusion of our exploration into the nuances of legacy and the profound impact of our choices, it becomes evident that the stories we leave behind are intricately woven into the fabric of time. Each decision we make, however small, reverberates through the lives of those who come after us, shaping their paths in ways we may never fully comprehend.

Reflections on legacy often evoke thoughts of monumental achievements, yet it is the collective tapestry of our everyday actions that primarily outlines our true impact. The kindness we extend to others, the values we uphold, and the wisdom we share become the threads that connect generations. Our legacy is not solely defined by the milestones we reach but by the echoes of our character, the lessons imparted, and the relationships forged along the way. In this ongoing journey, we are reminded that legacy is not merely a destination but a continuous journey. It is in the everyday moments that we find the true essence of our influence. A smile shared with a stranger, a listening ear offered in times of need, or a simple act of generosity can ripple outward, touching lives in ways we might never witness.

Moreover, our legacies are enriched by the diversity of experiences and perspectives we encounter. By embracing change and learning from each encounter, we cultivate a legacy of adaptability and open-mindedness, encouraging others to do the same. As we navigate the winding paths of existence, let us be conscious architects of our stories, weaving them with threads of empathy, courage, and hope.

The legacy we leave is a mosaic of our intentions, actions, and hopes—a testament to the values we cherish and the dreams we dare to pursue. Let us strive to craft legacies that inspire, uplift, and endure, lighting the way for those who will walk this earth long after we are gone.

In contemplating the legacies we cultivate, it's essential to recognize that life is a continual process of appeal—a series of choices, reflections, and their consequences. Each experience serves as a unique brushstroke on the canvas of who we are. Through triumphs and tribulations alike, we deepen our understanding of ourselves and our connections to others. By embracing our failures as opportunities for growth, we not only strengthen our character but also model resilience for future generations.

In this way, our lives become a living testament to the power of perseverance and the beauty of human imperfection. As we journey through the highs and lows, every scar and every smile adds depth and richness to our personal narrative, transforming us into a source of inspiration for those who follow.

Moreover, the legacies we build are not confined to grand gestures or monumental successes. They are equally composed of the quiet moments of introspection, the whispered encouragements, and the silent vows to be better. It is in these subtle, often overlooked instances that our true impact is forged. We teach others not just through our successes, but through our vulnerability and willingness to learn from mistakes.

Let us embrace the notion that our legacy is an evolving masterpiece, continuously shaped by our actions and intentions. As we paint our lives with compassion, authenticity, and courage, we invite others to contribute their own colors, creating a shared legacy of hope and transformation. In doing so, we ensure that the stories we leave behind are not merely chapters of our own lives but vibrant threads in the larger tapestry of humanity.

The choices we make today resonate far beyond our immediate surroundings. They are the seeds sown in the hearts and minds of those who follow, nurturing a landscape of values, perspectives, and inspirations. As we navigate the complexities of life, let us remain mindful of the legacies we are crafting—recognizing that even the simplest acts of compassion can yield profound, lasting change.

The beauty of our legacy lies not only in its grandeur but also in its subtlety—the quiet gestures that echo through time, leaving an indelible mark on the world. Every kind word, every thoughtful action, and every moment of understanding contributes to a legacy of grace and dignity.

As we journey through life, let us remember that our influence extends far beyond what we can see. Our actions today are the foundation upon which future generations will build, and the ideals we champion will guide them long after we are gone. In this ever-evolving story of humanity, we are both the authors and the characters, shaping a narrative that is rich with the themes of love, empathy, and hope.

Let us be vigilant in our resolve to act with integrity and purpose, knowing that our legacy is woven from the tapestry of our daily lives. In embracing this responsibility, we become the architects of a future filled with promise and possibility—where the echoes of our compassion and wisdom continue to inspire and elevate those who come after us.

As we conclude this exploration, let us reaffirm our commitment to living with intention, knowing that our actions hold the power to shape not just our lives but the very future of humanity. In the grand tapestry of existence, may we aspire to leave behind legacies defined by love, understanding, and a deep sense of shared humanity—a legacy that endures across time, inspiring countless others to reflect, learn, and continue the cycle of growth.

May our journey be one of continuous learning and boundless compassion, where each step we take is guided by the light of our values and the strength of our convictions. Let us cherish the opportunities to connect, to uplift, and to empower, recognizing that every interaction is a chance to contribute to the collective tapestry of human experience.

In this interconnected world, the impact of our choices extends beyond borders and generations. By embracing empathy and courage, we can foster a culture of understanding and resilience—a world where differences are celebrated and common ground is sought with open hearts.

As we move forward, let us hold dear the wisdom of those who came before us while courageously forging new paths for those who will follow. In doing so, we become stewards of a legacy that is not only ours but belongs to all of humanity. Together, let us build a future that resonates with the harmonious echoes of shared dreams and aspirations, a testament to the enduring power of kindness and hope.

Chapter 14

In Summary:

In summary, "The Appeals Court of Life" serves as a thought-provoking exploration of the complex interplay between our choices, the concept of justice, and the quest for a fulfilling existence. By framing life's decisions within a legal context, the narrative not only highlights the weight of our actions but also encourages readers to reflect on their own paths and the inherent search for meaning. Ultimately, this book challenges us to recognize that our lives are continually subject to evaluation and that the pursuit of understanding ourselves and our decisions is a deeply personal and ongoing journey.

Through its unique approach, the book invites introspection, urging us to consider the broader implications of our daily decisions and how they shape the narrative of our lives. It suggests that each choice we make is akin to a case presented in the court of our conscience, where we are both the defendant and the judge.

This introspective journey is beautifully woven with moments of vulnerability, triumph, and realization, making the reader ponder the nuances of morality and the impact of their choices on the tapestry of their life's journey.

As we navigate through the intricacies of this metaphorical courtroom, we are reminded that personal growth and enlightenment are not destinations but rather ongoing processes that enrich our understanding of what it means to live a life of purpose and integrity.

Chapter 15

CLOSING ARGUMENT

The Final Appeal

Ladies and gentlemen of the jury of life,

We have heard the testimony of conscience. We have examined the evidence of choices made in shadow and light. We have weighed mercy against justice and legacy against regret. And now, as the gavel nears its final descent, we must ask ourselves, what verdict shall we render on the life we've lived?

The Appeals Court of Life is not a place of condemnation—it is a sanctuary of reflection. Here, every soul is given the chance to revisit its record, to appeal not for perfection, but for redemption. The judge presiding is not blind but compassionate. Not distant but deeply invested in the restoration of every heart that dares to hope.

Like Ellie the Elephant, we've stumbled through the jungle of our days—mud-splattered, dream-distracted, and sometimes hilariously off course. But in the laughter that follows the fall, we find grace. In the willingness to rise again, we find growth. And in the courage to appeal for a new chapter, we find the very heartbeat of redemption.

So let this be your final appeal—not to erase the past, but to embrace the future. To live not in fear of judgment, but in pursuit of wisdom. To walk forward, knowing that the court of grace is always in session.

Case closed. Life reopened.

Dr. Charles E. Cravey, August 2025

OTHER BOOKS BY DR. CRAVEY MAY BE FOUND AT:

https://drcharlescravey.com or Amazon.com

www.ingramcontent.com/pod-product-compliance
Lightning Source LLC
Chambersburg PA
CBHW030023290326
41934CB00005B/465